Wayward

Rebecca Addams

BookLeaf Publishing

India | USA | UK

Presentation by *BookLeaf Publishing*

Web: www.bookleafpub.com

E-mail: info@bookleafpub.com

ISBN: 9789360946784

First edition 2024

Love to my fellow islanders, who gave me
room to grow

PREFACE

Maybe I'm supposed to be professional, and talk about my inspiration, or what I intended to convey here with my random assortment of scribblings. This is my first time actually publishing anything I've written. I'd be remiss to tell you what to glean, as 'beauty is in the eye', and every artist would prefer their work to speak for itself. I will say, these words helped to heal me, and I hope they may do the same for someone else

—

He was there to plant the seed

that sprouted dark and thorny thing

which plucked me from my wide-eyed dream

and held aloft, then broke the wings
~

The Void

I'm just a bleeding-heart masochist
Here at your service
Breaking myself down for you is my purpose
When you reach out to me I feel that much less
worthless
I'll do what I can, though I doubt you deserve it
And I deserve someone who sees what my worth
is
But I'll bend to my breaking point while you
observe this
Desperate attempt to fill the gaps where my soul
splits
Walking a tightrope over the precipice
Falling away like sand into the abyss

Wealth

Those rare gems that light up my soul are my
dearest treasures.

You are glittering, golden, a dazzling canvas of
colors.

You do not see this.
You are unhewn,
uncut and
unpolished.
You are wild and rough,
sharp and hard.
I see where you shine.
It caught my eye from a distance,
and drew me in.
Like an explorer of old,
I chased a promise of beauty and reward, and
coming upon you,
it was found to be true.

I will never doubt your value,
even if you don't see it for yourself.
~

Sucker

Always willing, never no,

Never time to take it slow

No time to waste, you're far away

Yet, loving you cuts too much to stay

I know you never wanted me

But you always want me to bleed

and prove to you my loyalty

collecting favors like a fee

But you can barely look at me

If I'm a friend and not a vessel

Why is it I always wrestle

Between sense of duty and compassion

Dressed myself in such a fashion

Hardly recognize myself

Always chasing empty wealth

Put me back up on the shelf

Until the next time you need help

I'm a lifeline, I'm a raft,
I'm a rope when yours has snapped

Faithful crutch, I'll prop you up
Your weight will never be too much

Spending my life in the corner
Gathering dust and falling over
~

Infection

I have filled pages and pages
with words that
I will never say to you.

The heaviest kind of silence.

To bear it, and know that you will never feel its
weight.

To let it go, and watch it sink away into a distant
memory

This is the last bit of you
that is left in me
like an infection
So nondescript
it doesn't even merit a name

If you were a house
you'd be
unpainted
particleboard
I'd watch you
blow away in the wind

The truth is penicillin
Love, my panacea
I will sweat you out like a fever,
and from this point on,
you'll have to show up
in order to haunt me.
~

Inclement

He had not missed me.

I doubt I would've missed me, either.

No one ever misses a disaster.

Nobody longs for a hurricane or
fondly recalls memories of earthquakes or
wishes that a tornado would come back
and stay a while

I am a lightning storm
I roll with the wind

When I kiss the earth
It trembles

It is not my nature
to return

To keep me

You must
Ground me and
never

let me go
To begin with
~

Medusa

Time well spent, or wishful thinking?
Maybe you're not the hero I'm dreaming

Could this spidersilk thread be sustained?
Are you the one prophesized?
Can you walk through flame?
Is there a garden in your heart?
Is it filled with stone?
Will you stay, and leave me all alone?

I'm exhausting and difficult
Too loud, too much
Too me

Maybe I'll always be ready
for you to
disengage
tap out
hang it up
at any moment
especially the difficult ones

So few have found a reason to stay
that wasn't self-serving
and devoid of love.

When I have nothing to offer
but my own cup,
your thirst will be slaked
and your belly filled;

Yet my love earns no devotion
and the taste, sickly sweet,
brings on
Madness
Pain
Petrification

I want to leave this graveyard island
But I'm a poor swimmer
and my only friends are sharks
~

The Maze

To face down your demons,
You've got to free them
The only way out is through
Turn by turn, deeper you'll find
The Minotaur in the Maze is you

~

I must prepare to do battle
(Like Buffy? Or Waymond?)
Can one stake a shadow?
Could one love a demon?

Appointed GOA
of the revolution
The enemy, fully aware
that I'm clueless
I can't hold a gun,
let alone shoot it,
but I'm told
"The only way out is through this"
Even Hercules needed
Olympian assistance

Have you ever
gone to war

with yourself?
The enemy
knows your moves
all too well
Still, you're evenly matched;
Go give 'em hell

~

Breaststroke

On a good day,
I can stand in faith
like a gentle stream,
wade in up to my knees,
and let it usher me
towards that blissful destination
where all things flow.

Some days
I cannot find my footing,
and I slip-
bash my heart
on jagged stone,
and come up with lungs
full of doubt and fear.

I am not a strong swimmer.

Perhaps you could build me a raft
so that the only body
I fall in
will be
love
~

Doubt

Spitting mad with a venom tongue

Teeth clench around primal fear that
You were just another lie
That everything I wanted
  didn't want me.

But you proved it true, didn't you?

I still haven't read your last message.
I can't promise that I will.
As long as I don't, I am insulated.
Schrodinger's heartbreak;
I may hope and wonder equally,
and each will torment just the same.

What need have I of an answer?

What need have I of an answer!

What need have I of a certain answer.

Nothing is certain but death, taxes, and my
unyielding love of you.

What a joke!
What a lie.
What a farce.
What great missteps
    we make with our hearts

My heart is an empty room,
with ghosts posed as furniture

Silence is deafening in liminal spaces
The echo travels farther than the scream

Days ago I thought that I could face this
with my head held high and a regal sort of grace,
but-

God may not wish to share a crown
with a stubborn spoiled bitch like me.
    ~

Tide

The red tide rolled in this morning,
Tinting every boone with fear.
Bells and sirens scream from the shore.
To my deafened ears, hardly a threat

The world has been flooded and I am adrift,
somewhere- a tiny, bright speck
in a massive black, churning ocean.

Upgrade from a raft to a rowboat.
I can steer now, for whatever that's worth.
At the moment, it couldn't matter less.
I don't know how to navigate by stars.

But I'm here, and I'm still alive.
I will not breathe salt water
I will thrash and gasp and reach for the surface.
I will find something solid to pull myself up
with
out of the murky water, and into the
warmth of the sun.

I may be a poor sailor now.
Perhaps one day I'll have the makings of a poor
Captain.

~

Bejeweled

I am beautiful. smart. funny. compassionate.
creative. eternally optimistic. positively
relentless.

I am a catch,
a snack,
the full fucking package

It may seem arrogant to say,
But its taken this long just to
like my own skin,
let alone
see its worth.

So I will loudly proclaim,
for no benefit but my own,
just how worthy I am.

I will never forget the untold treasures I have to
offer. I will hold them up in my heart and never
again be tempted to grant thieves and charlatans
safe passage.

My temple is alive with repulsion.
Every booby trap, another warning.

Turn back.
You can't hack it.
You don't have what it takes.

Until some day,
my personal Indiana Jones
will lay siege to my cache and
make off with the best of me,
because he'll have what it takes
to bypass every pitfall,
dodge projectiles and
solve every puzzle to
Reach me
and lift me out of there.
~

Flight

Oh, my sweet fledgling,

What are you so afraid of?

I'm not quite harmless,
but certainly not dangerous

and you, precious,

still downed and half-blind,

are walking yourself in circles
over when can you finally fly?

Be at peace.
Eat.
Grow.

When you're ready, your wings will open
themselves.

~

Streams

There is a river behind my eyes
It flows undamned over
the
cliff
face
with
abandon
eager to taste flight
be moved to foreign lands
find itself changed
into
a pool
a rapids
a lake

There is an Ocean
in my heart
deep as Mariana
and who could hope to drain the sea?

I carry life to barren shores
Harbor fantastic and terrible secrets
Rage in the tide of the Moon
Ferry foolhardy men to sandy graves

Keep life and death laced together like a lock of
hair in a jewelry box

Merciless and
Nurturing

It all depends on your vessel
and how deep
you choose
to dive
~

Pt. 2

____

"It's my fault and I'm just going to leave it
there."

Leave me there too, while you're at it.

You leave me anywhere you drop me
and expect me to just be waiting there

But I'm a river, baby,
I don't wait- I roll

If I held your place, you'd be
blocking my flow

If you want to try to dam me up,
Then you've gotta go

It's sink or swim, and mind the undertow

I've only got time for
flowing, streaming, splashing
You want to drip me through a faucet
Trapped in prison made of plastic

You want domain over an evanescent entity
Like an ant laying claim to a puddle
Like a ship that hopes to own the Ocean

Not realizing that I belong everywhere, to
everyone, and
have no allegiance to anything
under God
but that which I am charged with;

Which is simply
to flow
~

Soiled

You left me in this pit.
I called out to you, with reaching hands.
You offered a bucket of dirt
Every time you said,
I'm smart
(why can't you do this)
I'm tough
(you'll get over it)
I can handle it
(just smile)
I can do anything
(except that. or that)

I brought you my dreams like dandelion tufts.
You called them weeds and blew them away
without a wish in your heart for me but to stop
collecting flowers.

You have buried me
in your denigration;
Sand in my eyes and dust in my lungs
Stones in my belly
my mouth
my ears

I will be a seed

I will be a sculptor

I will make clay
from tears and burial dirt
I will build a staircase, a trellis
I will build a wall around my plot

I will rise like a garden
Bask in the sun
Drink in the rain
Give refuge to bees and butterflies

Keep your dust and muck
You can lay in it, make dirt angels
Make mud into cement shoes
You will never make a garden
You don't know about water and sunlight
How to prune and protect
something so delicate
as a flower
~

Peaking

Near the abyss
Tread lightly
A sheer drop

But the impact
isn't nearly as bad
as the waiting
throat dry from screaming
eyes welded shut with your own tears
torched by the wind,
deafening and
relentless

The sight of the horizon
drove me to dance
Ever the Fool,
I don't know how
to dance
gingerly

spinning
dizzy
my feet
kiss the edge
farewell

I couldn't tell you
what I felt
on my back

I was certain
they were wings
~

Unknown

You say you love the person I used to be

Who is that, I wonder?

The girl cradled in fear and isolation?
The girl who lived in alabaster?
The blind fool who stumbled her way through
life with outstretched hands, searching for
something always out of reach?
The girl who would gladly skin her knees and
crawl on broken glass just to hear a loving
word?

The girl who formed in sand and darkness
The girl with fire in her veins and
knives on her tongue
The girl who cut away pieces of herself
To be understood
To be accepted
To be loved

You say you miss her,
as if she was not the seed
who pushed through stone and
bloomed into the rose before you.

You curse her for her thorns,
as if she were ever the sort
to accept clumsy hands,
possession mistaken for adoration,
shears in favor of clippers.

As if her defenses weren't grown through sun
and rain, according to the design of nature.

As if there could never exist a better way to hold
her, love her, encourage her bloom

It takes a gardener to love a seedling
to water it every day like a prayer
trusting sun and soil and clockwork
without knowing for sure what it may grow into

A gardener would love no less a rose bush that
grew from a stony bed, despite no effort from
him.
~

Value

I am kintsugi,
baby.
I will take
the pieces you left me in
and make
something beautiful

I am an alchemist
I can transmute
pain into strength
defeat into resilience
hate into love
bitterness into compassion

I could take the bullshit you give me
and turn it into Gold, too.
But that's a waste of my gifts.
I've learned
the hard way
that the base materials
must be of good quality
in order to make
anything
worthwhile
~

Kingdoms

Perhaps
you are not
MY Emperor

Bright and gold
though your crown may be,
'tis casting shadows
on my Throne

I am the mirror;
you do not see
else but your own
countenance.
Your gaze is merely
surface-deep
I refuse the
however-ornate frame
you'd have me hanged in
I am not some
pretty headpiece
No demure, meek thing

I am a shield-maiden
  who charges into battle
I am Cleopatra in the carpet

I am Elizabeth, who holds her crown
I am Suiko, who carves a path
   and lights the way

"My place" is never on a wall
   ~

St. Rapunzel

It's time to leave the tower

I have left your precious idols in pieces
(better than any state you've left me in)

I could walk this earth twenty lifetimes and find
refuge in the jagged stone-
even as it cuts my soles-
So long as it's far away from you

You've quartered me with your contempt
What sort of soldier breaks so finely?
Perhaps the kind with poisoned blood
So that retribution may see you home
Crime and punishment as one, to compliment
your laurel bough.
Ride and tell your countrymen the deed that you
have done
While anima cast queer visions over battles lost
and won
I was not the beast you deemed, the Minotaur
you know
I am something you daren't dream, a greater
source of woe

~

Garden Bed

There was once a lovely garden
Where I was so blessed to be caged
I grew up easy in the sun
I danced in wind and played in rain
As years went by the walls closed in
Thorn and thistle, overgrown
Though I loved my garden,
I could no longer call it home
Weeds twisted into my bed
There birds refused to perch
One day with a heavy heart
I set out on a search
With foolish feet and heart for guides,
We tread what road we came upon
Never caring for direction
We saw fit to chase the sun
Now I have swam the deepest oceans
I have climbed the tallest mountains
I have stood on melting earth
I drank life from every fountain
I ran with wolves and flew with birds
Wandered plains with untold herds
No matter where I laid my head,
My thoughts were of my garden bed
~